Dedication

Abby and Alyssa are real people. They both have significant medical challenges and use sign language to talk. As growing sisters, their energy and charisma can be inspirational to anyone that wishes to learn.

This series of books is dedicated to Abby and Alyssa who inspire me, and to Grandma Gina who lives on within our hearts.

Grandpa Don

Hi! My name is Abby and this is my sister Alyssa.

Alyssa uses signs instead of words to talk. She makes these signs with her hands.

You already know some signs like waving your hand to say hi.

Come with us to the zoo and we'll learn more signs!

Hi: Open hand waved side to side.

There are signs for many things, like "zoo".

Let's see what animals we can find and sign them together!

Zoo: With a pointed finger, trace a "Z" in front of the body that ends in the "O" sign.

What animal is that?

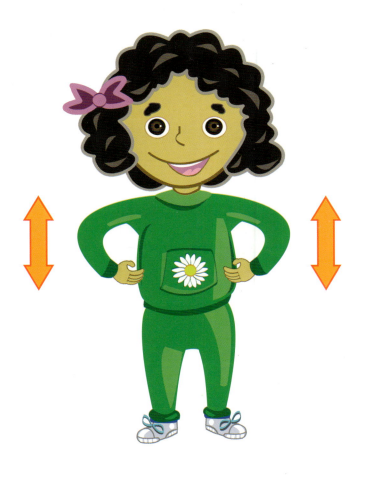

The Sign: With curved hands, scratch both sides upward twice.

That's right, it's a monkey!

Let's all make the sign for a monkey.

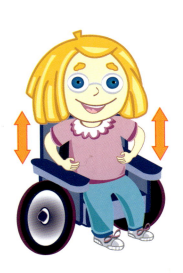

Monkey: With curved hands, scratch both sides upward twice.

What animal is that?

The Sign: Cross wrists of clawed hands and scratch up and down near each shoulder twice.

That's right, it's a bear!

Let's all make the sign for a bear.

Bear: Cross wrists of clawed hands and scratch up and down near each shoulder twice.

What animal is that?

The Sign: Move the right "C" hand, palm facing in, from in front of chin upward in front of the face.

Let's all make the sign for a giraffe.

Giraffe: Move the right "C" hand, palm facing in, from in front of chin upward in front of the face.

Let's all make the sign for an elephant.

Elephant: Use a bent "B" hand against the nose, palm down, move hand downward and forward, with a large wavy movement.

What animal is that?

The Sign: Starting with the right curved "5" hand pointing down over the forehead, palm in, move hand back over the top of the head.

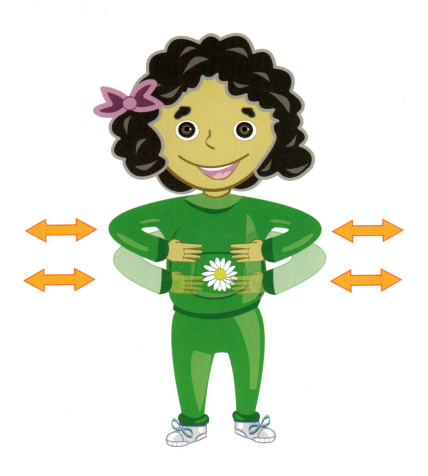

The Sign: "4" sign both hands, palms in, tips facing. Place over chest and draw apart. Lower to waist and repeat.

That's right, it's a zebra!

Let's all make the sign for a zebra.

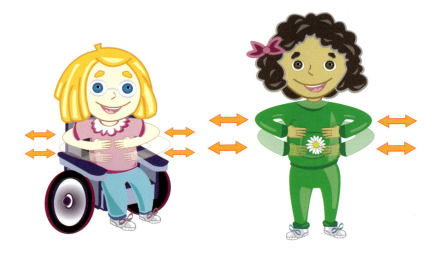

Zebra: "4" sign both hands, palms in, tips facing. Place over chest and draw apart. Lower to waist and repeat.

Let's all make the sign for a wolf.

We've learned the signs for a lot of animals today.

It's time for Alyssa and me to go home...

Let's all make the sign for good-bye!

Good-Bye: Wave open hand up and down.

For more fun with sign language, you can practice your A,B,C's and numbers!

alphabet

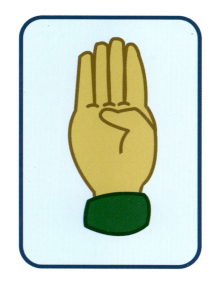

A   **B**

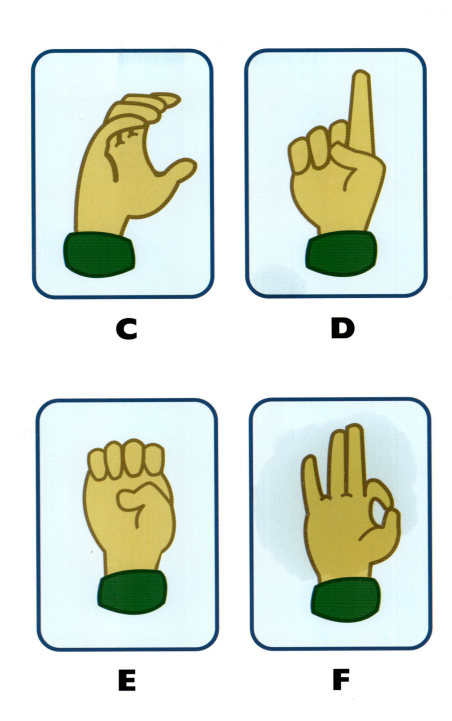

C

D

E

F

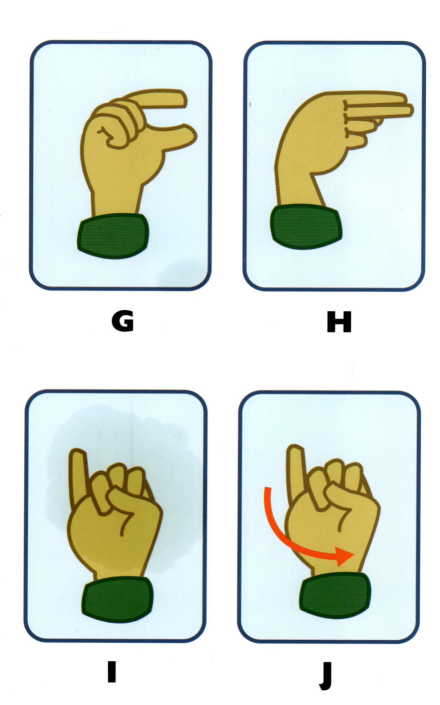

G

H

I

J

K

L

M

N

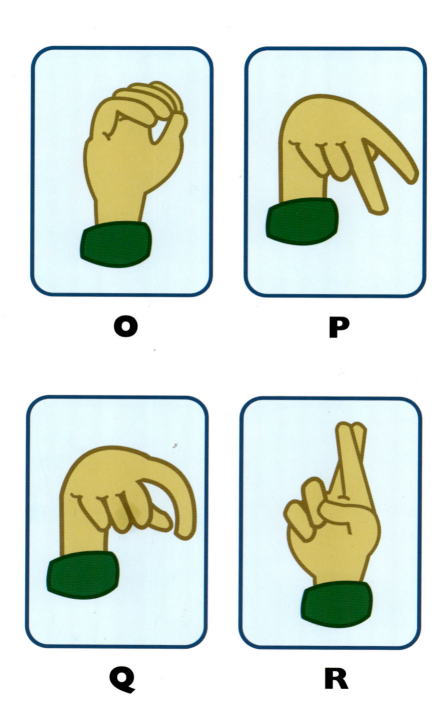

O

P

Q

R

S

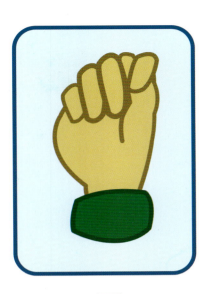

T

U

V

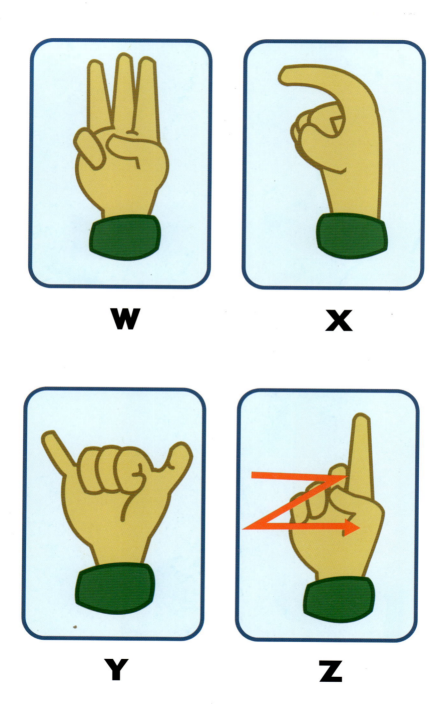

W

X

Y

Z

numbers 1 - 10

1

2

3

4

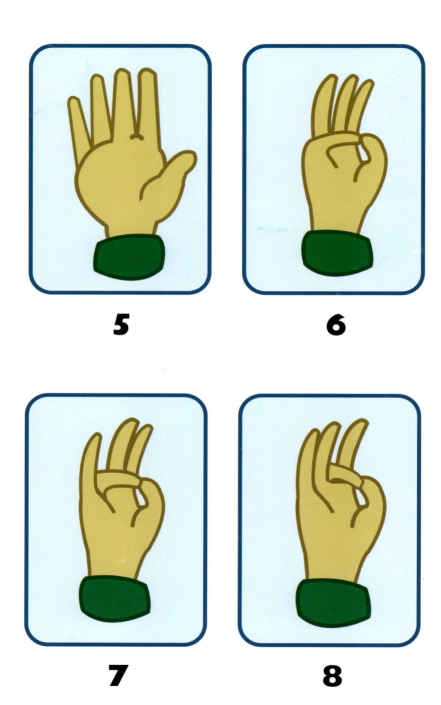

5

6

7

8

9

10

Acknowledgements

Some words in sign language have multiple acceptable signs. In those instances where multiple signs were available, Grandpa Don chose the sign most appropriate for Abby and Alyssa.

Grandpa Don encourages readers who want to learn more about sign language to read:

• "The Art of Sign Language" by
   Christopher Brown; Random House.

• "Webster's Unabridged American
   Sign Language Dictionary" by Elaine Costello, PHD.

And to also visit these websites:

• www.signingsavvy.com

• www.lessontutor.com